LEADERS

JEFF HARRIS, D. Min.

Acknowledgement

To George and Lynda Harris,

Growing up in your home taught me about sacrificial leadership and enduring resolve toward a cause greater than one's self. I am humbled by your tireless and enthusiastic encouragement and indebted to your selfless and steadfast love.

Your son,
Jeff

Introduction

→ → → → → → → → → → → → → →

A Process

My shelves are layered with book after book on leadership! So many books on leadership and so few on the *process*. This material is an attempt to take the great leadership principles gleaned from many great leadership idea books and put them into a process that will allow emerging leaders to sharpen and hone their leadership skills.

In 1994, I made one of the great decisions of my life. As a 26-year-old pastor with responsibility well beyond my experience, I knew I needed to grow in leadership. I made a commitment to learn and grow as a leader. Since then, I have benefited much from the principles of leadership, but with a growing church I faced a growing challenge: how do I raise leaders and multiply? Do I simply provide a bibliography full of great books on leadership and hope they all digest, assimilate and employ leadership principles? After wrestling with this, I realized the real need was an effective leadership principle application *process*.

This application process is approached as four areas covered in this material:

- *Foundational Leadership*: What do you, as an individual, need to discover and determine to be personally effective?

- *Self-Leadership*: What must I do to continue to grow as a leader throughout my life?

- *Team Leadership*: How do I apply what I have learned and develop sound leadership at the group level?

- *Multiplying Leadership*: How do I identify, develop and deploy leaders in an organization?

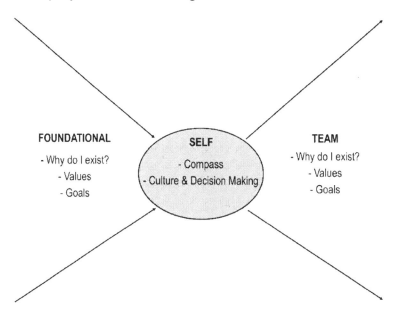

FOUNDATIONAL

- Why do I exist?
- Values
- Goals

SELF

- Compass
- Culture & Decision Making

TEAM

- Why do I exist?
- Values
- Goals

The Leadership Forum Experience

You are going through this material because someone identified you a person who is either leading, has led or are viewed as a person who has the capacity to lead (an emerging leader). You are here by invitation because your leadership matters. Do not underestimate the Leadership Forum experience.

Experience

Leadership Forum is a survey of the field of leadership. It involves a workbook which facilitates discussion, application and the practice of leadership development principles. It is best experienced in a small group where there is a few minutes of teaching, lots of discussion and homework assignments in between. This material is interactive, introspective and personal.

Benefit
Leadership Forum is intended to dial in your own leadership lens at a personal level and fan all the way out to macro leadership across teams. It will challenge you to wrestle with your personal mission, life purpose and values. It will push you to be intentional and effective in how you lead others forward and to confront your own hurdles in getting there. It is the kind of experience that becomes an asset in every season of life in any context—church, work, family.

Expectations
Leadership Forum is best experienced in a small group that is attended consistently, while engaging the material between sessions. You are also expected to invest in other leaders by leading another person (or more) through the material when you are finished. The process hinges upon application.

You determine the value of this experience for yourself and your peers based upon how willing you are to be authentic in re-examining areas of your life along the way. Your participation in group discussions and readiness to apply lessons to real life is critical. If you do these things, you will get a lot out of this and it will bear fruit in your family, work, social and ministry contexts. Leadership Forum is a great way to invest in your leadership development journey. Get ready to dive in!

~Pastor Jeff Harris

Table of Contents

FOUNDATIONAL LEADERSHIP

LESSON ONE: Why Do I Exist?

→ → → → → → → → → → → → → →

The Call to Lead

The age old question in leadership circles is whether or not leadership is born or learned. From a biblical perspective leadership is born, learned and most importantly "called." Every believer is on some level responsible to lead. The Great Commission calls each of us to be disciple makers. This very notion implies that we will be teaching and developing someone else. From a spiritual standpoint it is important to understand that since we are temples of the Holy Spirit we will influence others.

J.O. Sanders states in *Spiritual Leadership*, "No one can be neutral, either morally or spiritually. On lives that come within the range of our influence we leave an indelible impress, whether we are conscious of it or not."

Several years ago I had a neighbor approach me while I was mowing my grass on a Saturday afternoon. He commented, "Every Saturday you are out here mowing your grass, how do you do that? I thought most pastors studied on Saturdays." I told him that I had made a commitment to do my sermon prep early in the week so that I had time to be with my family and help my wife. Several months later his wife commented to my wife the change they experienced in their own home based on the conversation that her husband had.

You lead by means of influence everywhere you go, the real

question is: do you lead well?

Can you think of a time you influenced someone and didn't know it until much later? What opportunities do these represent?

How are influence and leadership the same? How are they different? How do you move from possessing influence to exerting leadership?

*Leadership is the capacity to
translate vision into reality.*
(Warren Bennis)

Read 1 Corinthians 6:19-20. What are the implications of this passage for you, how you live, how you plan and how you lead?

List here the people, teams, and organizations that you have had the opportunity to influence.

The Gifts to Lead

Scripture teaches that leadership is a 'spiritual gift' and those who possess this gift should us it with diligence. "He who leads, lead with diligence" (Romans 12:8). The question becomes, "if I don't have the spiritual gift of leadership, am I responsible or capable of leading?" The answer is absolutely! While not all of us possess the spiritual "gift" of evangelism, scripture makes it clear we are to evangelize—each and every one of us. And while we may not possess the endowed ability to lead, we certainly *can* and *must* lead in certain situations.

Identify situations in which you lead. Describe the way in which you channel influence to intentionally lead people in these contexts.

As a parent:

In your church:

In your workplace:

In the community:

make the most of every opportunity. (Colossians 4:5)

The Character to Lead

Nominal leadership and great leadership are largely differentiated by *character*. Great leadership possesses character at high levels. Certain character traits are essential for effective leadership.

Read each character trait and the scripture passage associated with it.

- Character: integrity (is), ethos (perceived)
    Psalm 78:72—Leadership requires integrity.

- Positive Desire: attitude (mindset), passion (vigor)
    Psalm 119:139—Leadership requires
    positive/passionate attitude.

- Teachability: life learner (pursuer), coachable (receiver)
    Proverbs 1:8—Leadership means being
    teachable.

- Influence: magnetism (draws), followers (retains)
    Matthew 4:19-20—Leadership implies followers.

- Discipline: consistent practices (sustainable), daily (resolve)
    Luke 9:23—Leadership requires discipline.

Exercise: Solicit feedback from at least 5 people on which of these 5 domains you have the greatest growth opportunity or challenge in. Seek diverse input from family, co-workers, ministry partners, and friends to get a well-rounded survey of your own Character to Lead profile. Self-assess before surveying others so next week you can share contrast between self-perceived and externally perceived characteristics. Begin this exercise right away so that you have adequate responses before the next session!

What are your greatest opportunities for growth?

Record the responses you received from others regarding your character to lead growth opportunity areas here.

How different are they from your self-perception as a leader?

Do you see any correlation between the perception and the context from which people were evaluating you?

Do you see how deficiencies in any of these domains can undermine your capacity to effectively lead?

Every leader or leadership situation has one thing in common. That is *purpose*. Where leadership is expressed there is a purpose in mind. Each example shows how an ultimate purpose was the motivation behind the leadership given.

What was the purpose of Martin Luther King, Jr.?

What was the purpose of Billy Graham?

What is the purpose of a parent?

If one does not know to which port
he is sailing, no wind is favorable.
(Seneca)

You've got to be careful if you don't
know where you're going, because
you might not get there!
(Yogi Bera)

Developing a Purpose Statement

Alfred Nobel dropped the newspaper and put his head in his hands. Nobel was a Swedish chemist who made his fortune inventing and producing dynamite. It was 1888 and his brother Ludvig had died in France.

But now Alfred's grief was compounded by dismay. He'd just read an obituary in a French newspaper—not his brother's obituary, but his! An editor has confused these brothers. The headline read, "The Merchant of Death is Dead." Alfred Nobel's obituary described a man who had gotten rich by helping people kill one another.

Shaken by this appraisal of his life, Nobel resolved to use his wealth to change his legacy. When he died eight years later, he left more than $9 million to fund awards for people whose work benefited humanity. The awards became known as the Nobel Prize.

Alfred Nobel had a rare opportunity—to look at the assessment of his life at its end and still have the chance to change it. (Alcorn, *The Treasure Principle*)

Great leaders are purpose oriented. In order to lead others well you must have a clear personal purpose. In order to develop your personal purpose statement, it is best to begin with the destination in mind. What that means is that you picture who you want to be at the end of your life by writing down what you want to have accomplished or would like to be said of you. One way in which to get at this is to write your obituary as you would like for it to be read.

Obituary

After completing your obituary, identify key aspects of what you would desire to best define your life and put that into a purpose statement

Purpose Statement

I exist to...

It's important for your purpose statement to be memorable and concise. Single sentence, no paragraphs; something that would be never-changing and an engine for all arenas of life.

Write your purpose statement in a single sentence:

Verbally communicating your purpose statement commits you. It makes it concrete. Share your purpose statement with someone important to you. Share it also with the group.

A value of your purpose statement is that it prioritizes you, it obligates you and it will serve to hold you accountable. If we were sailing to Fiji from Houston we would know our destination and any coordinates that were not consistent with arriving at that destination would be clear. Should our compass reveal we are off course, when we could make a course correction? If we didn't have a specified destination, we wouldn't know if we were off course. The difference between sailing and drifting has everything to do with your defined destination.

Based on your Purpose Statement, are you on course?

Developing Resolutions

A helpful tool to keep you on course and ensure your arrival at your envisioned destination is a resolution. A resolution answers the questions, "What must I do in order to arrive at the destination?" <u>A resolution is a pathway</u>. Based upon your purpose statement there will emerge clear areas of your life that must receive special attention in order for you to arrive at your destination. For instance, if your purpose statement says, "I exist to love my family, etc…" then a compatible resolution would be, "then I must spend time with my family." While this is a simple example, it demonstrates the relationship between a resolution and your purpose statement.

Resolutions are the main ingredients in your leadership recipe. On the way to your destination, you can see certain mile markers. These are your resolutions.

Resolutions are different from goals (which we will deal with later). Resolutions are life-long while goals are dynamic, changing over time. Resolutions are related to purpose and are fixed points that are clear at all times. Resolutions should be few. *In order to fulfill my purpose, I will…*

Resolutions will expand as you do, but they do not change in principle. For example, when my kids are grown and have families of their own, I would expand my resolution to my role as a grandparent, but the principle of being a spiritual leader to my family is still retained.

Resolutions

I exist to… Therefore, I must…

Notes:

LESSON TWO: The Importance of Values

→ → → → → → → → → → → → → → →

Values Guide Your Behavior

One of the easiest ways to determine what you value is to look at your actions. Another way is to identify your pet peeves. The characteristics or actions of others that tend to annoy you are the converse of that which you value. Values often fall somewhere along a continuum of aspirational-actual-exasperational.

Identify some of your values. What do your actions and behavior reveal? What do you appreciate and affirm?

What brings you angst? Can you identify from your pet peeves what you value? Are they the same?

Make a list of your top ten values and any corresponding scripture.

1. _____

2. _____

3. _____

4. _____

5. _____

6. _____

7. _____

8. _____

9. _____

10. _____

Values Define What is Essential

Values are the DNA of a person, family and team. Much like team colors, our values tell what is essential to us and reveals to others what is essential. Values define who belongs—who has our DNA. Values are often times the unspoken force in a team, family or company. Someone who is new to the team, family or company will quickly learn what we do and don't do around here. Values that are unstated are often confusing and alienating for those who are new to the family, team or organization.

My wife's family had the habit of eating off of one another's plates. They value sharing. I'm the youngest of four and if you touch my plate you might get a fork in your arm! I had to learn the hard way not to fight for my food the first time I had a family meal with my wife's side of the family. My desire to belong, to be a part of the family challenged me to evaluate my values and embrace a new set of values. In a company setting someone who persists in not sharing the values of the company is soon no longer with the company. Values determine who belongs.

Have you ever been in a situation where you discovered a company's, family's or team's unstated values? How did it feel?

Why is it important to clearly state your values?

Synergy of Purpose and Values

Purpose tells us what we are going to do and values tell us the way in which we are going to go about fulfilling that purpose.

"The end does not justify the means!"

"The journey is as important as the destination."

Say, for example, my destination (purpose) may be to drive my family to South Padre Island for a vacation. If my values aren't clearly stated, then going from point A to point B is what matters. I can honk in the driveway, gripe that there it too much luggage, and refuse to stop for potty breaks. If, however, I have a value of unity and family intimacy, then my values will affect my behavior. The way in which I pursue the destination (purpose) will be affected by my values.

Do you see the difference between your purpose and your values?

How will your values affect your pursuit of the purpose of your life?

Aligning Values

Not only do values provide our DNA, that is who belongs, but they serve as an alignment tool. Values are celebrated and rewarded, recognized and reproved. Everyone wants to know where the bell is located in order to ring it. When values are clearly defined they need to be enforced. In your development of personal values, you need to see the inherent reward or cost associated with your values.

What is the reward to living out the value of family intimacy on your vacation trip?

What is the cost of NOT living out the value of family intimacy on your vacation trip?

The Values Disconnect

We should value what God values. Where there are disconnects we should strive God-ward. As Christ followers, it is essential that our values be Godly values. There are numerous values in scripture, and it is important that the values we develop be consistent with those of God. *Value is worship.*

Worship actually means to ascribe worth to someone or something. When our values are Godly values, then we are actually worshipping because we are ascribing worth to what God says is valuable.

On your list of personal values, which (if any) are not consistent with God's values?

What values do you want to exemplify but do not currently?

What value will you have the hardest time living out?

What accountability can you put in place in order to live out this value? What does that look like?

Establishing Values Through Practice

Read Genesis 32:22-32.

Jacob walked with a limp and because of his experience, and the children of Israel didn't eat the meat of the hip ever since. **Why is this significant?**

This is truly a spiritual marker for Jacob, but the ongoing practice of not eating the meat from this area commemorates the name change to Israel and it commemorates God's blessing. One of the ways we value something is to commemorate it through our daily practice.

- The value of *faith*, might be commemorated with daily family prayer

- The value of *encouragement*, could be commemorated with a "you are special" plate during family meals

- The value of *trust*, could be commemorated by assigning individual responsibilities to family members

Do you see how each of these represents an opportunity to daily live out and enforce your values? What are some ways to craft expressions, reinforcements of, displays of your selected values?

Daily Enforce Your Values

Rewrite your list by priority. Make additions and eliminations as needed.

1. _____

2. _____

3. _____

4. _____

5. _____

6. _____

7. _____

8. _____

9. _____

10. _____

1. Take five values and establish your own working definition.

2. Add a "tag line" or a "catch phrase" to make it memorable.

3. Develop a practice by which the value can be incorporated and reinforced:

1. _____

_____

_____

2. _____

_____

_____

3. _____

_____

_____

4. _____

_____

_____

5. _____

_____

_____

What are some ways you could daily incorporate your values into your life?

Notes:

LESSON THREE: Goal Setting

→ → → → → → → → → → → → → →

Effort, Time and Energy

The momentum required to succeed takes an incredible amount of effort, time and energy. Jesus ministered for three years under duress and difficult circumstances. His ultimate goal was our salvation, but He had several other incremental goals: to preach the kingdom, call the disciples and establish the church. These incremental goals were prerequisites or stage-setting to accomplish his overall purpose. You must have specific goals in order to arrive at your destination.

Fulfilling Your Resolutions Through Goals

Resolutions are the obvious criteria for you to successfully reach your destination. You can see them from here! Goals are strategic processes implemented to achieve and pursue the resolution. Since the resolution is in relationship to the destination (purpose), it is timeless. Goals are related to the pursuit of the resolution. They should change as they are achieved.

Goals are a strategic tool used to achieve and pursue the resolutions that lead to your destination. If the resolution is physical fitness then a goal may be to run two miles, four days a week in twenty minutes. The resolution stays the same but the goal will change as it is achieved or re-evaluated. It is a superimposed strategic tool to help assist you in getting to your destination. When you radically change your life towards the goal you make your way towards your destination (fulfilling your purpose).

Evaluate your current life process. What does it look like day to day? Do you presently have any goals you are pursuing?

How do you set goals? How do you know if you have good goals that will get you to your resolutions?

Vision without implementation
is hallucination.
(Benjamin Franklin)

Make SMARTY goals: specific,
measurable, achievable, realistic,
time-oriented, and yours.

Goal Setting

The Mapping Process
Make the relationship between your goals and resolutions visible.

Resolutions "I exist to...Therefore I will..."

Goals "I will get there by..."

- Each goal has definable, measurable, time-oriented outcome: how will we know if this goal is effective?

    Example: I will run two miles under twenty minutes, four times a week to increase cardio strength, loose ten pounds and lower cholesterol 30 points within four months.

- Each goal has a specific process: how will this goal be implemented?

    Example: I will run four days' week primarily at 7:30am weekdays on a neighborhood trail. I will use a treadmill on rainy days.

The Mastering Process
Make your goals better.

- Evaluate the design of your process.

    Example: After six weeks I will check my cholesterol and weight. If weight decreased and cholesterol lowered, it is successful thus far and should be ready to increase my distance or lower my time.

- Evaluate the implementation. Don't change your goal without faithfully implementing it first.

  > Example: If after six weeks my cholesterol is still high and my weight has not changed, I must evaluate my ability to execute the plan. Did I run four times a week? Did I run two miles? Did I run it under twenty minutes? If no, my plan may be fine, but the implementation might be poor.

  > *Leaders are not made in a day;*
  > *they are made daily.*
  > (John Maxwell)

The Momentum Process
Make goals increasingly dynamic.

- Start with big goals. Goals should be achievable but not without cost. Don't set your sights too low! Your goals should require significant change as well as sacrifice.

- Start with ruthless incremental consistency. This builds momentum.

- Expand upon arrival. When a goal is reached, we must change the goal and expand upon it in order to fulfill our resolutions.

The Metronome Process
Make your goals daily.

- Progress is made with pursuing your goals consistently, not sporadically.

What are your goals? List at least one goal for every resolution you have defined as necessary for fulfilling your purpose statement.

Embodying Your Purpose

Identify your excuse, reason, hurdle, circumstance or obstacle that stands between you and your destination (purpose). We each have road blocks we've allowed to justify non-progress. Name them.

Read Philippians 4:12-13. How is this passage connected to embodying and pursuing your purpose?

Today flows from your purpose, values and goals.

Your perfect day may not be reached each day, but based upon your goals and your values, what should each day consist of?

Map out your perfect day. What would it consist of? How would it embody your purpose and values lived out?

Read 2 Corinthians 4:7-10. Paul is writing this to a bunch of people on a mission encountering opposition. He himself had endured prison, beatings and conflict in pursuit of his purpose. How are these verses connected to embodying your purpose?

Today rises or falls on discipline and accountability. You must come to realize the interdependence between accountability, discipline and success.

Read Hebrews 10:24-25. This passage is written to a group of Christians who had grown complacent in the fundamentals. Without accountability and resilient pursuit, we all are inclined to drift away from the core things.

Who will hold you accountable to your goals and values?

Do they have access to the information? (checkbook, scale, employer, spouse, etc.)

What does this accountability look like? How regular? Who initiates?

Is this accountability detailed based on your destination (purpose), resolution and goals?

Notes:

SELF **LEADERSHIP**

→　→　→　→　→　→　→　→　→　→　→　→　→　→

LESSON FOUR: The Leadership Compass

→ → → → → → → → → → → → → →

Self-Leadership

Self-leadership is a crucial aspect of leading well. It is surprising to discover how many leaders spend so little time investing in their own leadership development. Some leaders who are "naturally" gifted seemingly get away with little or no development, while others plateau almost immediately. It is important for all leaders to realize that unless they are investing in their own development they are doomed to plateau or worse, crash!

The Principle of Self-Leadership is that you should spend about 50% of your leadership time on Self-Leadership. I know what you are thinking: where will I find the time? The question of whether I continue to bail water or plug the hole is perennial, but in Self-Leadership the answer is always plug the hole. You must decide whether you want to be an effective leader in a progressive and ongoing manner, or whether where you are today is as effective and as far as you are willing to go.

Ever notice when traveling on an airline how the pre-flight safety lecture always involves special instruction that "in the event of an emergency" parents are to first secure their own oxygen mask before tending to any children? It is not out of lack of care for the precious children aboard any flight, it is a sober acknowledgement that without adults who are alive those children don't stand a chance.

How much time do you spend on Self-Leadership?

How many books do you read per year dedicated to leadership enrichment?

What relationships do you have that are dedicated to Self-Leadership?

How much money do you spend on Self-Leadership?

Will you make the commitment to Self-Leadership?

You cannot lead where
you are not going.

Read Ecclesiastes 10:10

Once you have made the commitment to Self-Leadership, the initial task is developing your *Leadership Compass*. Your Leadership Compass is a series of areas that maintain the trajectory of your course. Each of these areas is crucial for you to closely monitor as you journey in leadership. I will break these areas into three major groupings: the Call, the Relationship and the Cost. Within each of these groupings are vital areas that must be monitored in order to effectively self-lead.

The Leadership Compass

1) The Call
The Call to lead is the fundamental foundation for all effective leadership. A leader who doesn't know he has been called to the particular task and location that he is leading is susceptible to burnout, lethargy or using that situation as a springboard to the next opportunity.

The Call to lead many times is the only thing that keeps you vigilant in pursuit of the purpose and destination. There are times when you are in opposition or face complex circumstances and you feel like quitting, and your Call is what keeps you going.

Are you called to your present leadership position or location? How are you sure?

How does that calling affect you when times are tough?

Within the Call to lead, the issue of giftedness comes into play. The question arises, "Am I effectively using and developing the gifts that I possess?" If we know that we are called, then we must consistently determine if we are utilizing our gifts effectively. This question will keep us honest. Many times I see ministers as well as business people who are working outside of their giftedness because they emerged as a "jack of all trades" early in the careers and now choose to micro manage out of a failure to develop robust self-leadership. Also the trap of working outside of one's giftedness has to do with success. Many leaders succeed to the point of leisure. How many successful businessmen retire early to spend their days in leisure? What about mega-church pastors who leave the pastorate to write? What about faithful servants who reach their peak earning years and now are hard to find? These are all related to calling and giftedness. We should utilize our gifts in keeping with our calling. The second aspect is that of developing one's gifts.

What are the God-gifts you possess?

Are you faithful to continue to grow and develop these gifts?

How are you going about developing these gifts?

2) *The Relationship*

The Relationship has to do with my relationship to God, myself and others. There are four areas: Heart, Vision, Character and People.

Heart:

Is your heart on fire for what you are doing? Do you have passion?

Vision:

Are you clear about where you are headed? Do you have a focus on the future?

Character:

Are you maintaining your integrity? Are you submitted to God and to maintaining accountability? When you ask others about your humility/pride, how do they respond? Are there necessary action steps in this area?

People:

Do you love people more or less now that you're in leadership? Do you immerse yourself in people or do you try to avoid people? Is your heart larger or smaller towards people?

3) The Cost

The third part of your Leadership Compass is the Cost. This includes Home, Achilles' Heel and Pace.

Home:

A leader's home is sacred. You will be diminished in your capacity to lead others if you are not effectively leading at home. There is a cost to your home in being a leader, but there is great cost to your leadership in general if you are not leading first and foremost at home. Your compass should regularly assess your personal leadership at home.

How is your home leadership/stewardship?

Achilles' Heel:

We all have an area of weakness and we must identify it. Is it your health? Do you overeat or smoke? Is it your desire? Do you fantasize about other women or covet possessions? Is it your ego? Are you argumentative? Defensive? Arrogant? As a leader, you must identify your Achilles' Heel and seek accountability to keep you honest and humble.

What's your Achilles' Heel?

Pace:

As a leader, we must find a pace that is sustainable. Too often we can neglect healthy patterns for physical, emotional and spiritual health. Are you exhausted? Are you emotionally tired or weary? Do you have a measurable pace? Can you anticipate when your pace will be more hectic or when you can take a vacation or break? Do you impulsively vacate and rest?

How is your pace?

Avoidance is like relational credit card abuse, just compounding the expense for a future due date.

Time is the currency of values, what's your ledger reveal?

If you dedicated 50% of your leadership time to Self-Leadership, how much time would be spent in the groups of Call, Relationship and Cost?

It is important to develop a plan to spend 50% of your leadership time on Self Leadership. That plan should include an evaluation mechanism called your Leadership Compass. This Compass should regularly evaluate your Call, Relationships and Cost. Visualize a dashboard. Your Leadership Compass is a dashboard with three gauges: Call, Relationships and Cost. At any time, you can look at your dashboard and get a feel for your level of self-leadership. You should invest in developing these areas and add the investment tools to the plan.

What is your Self-Leadership Plan?

Notes:

LESSON FIVE: Leadership Culture and Decision Making

→ → → → → → → → → → → → → →

The Leadership Culture in You

Self-Leadership is painful at times. Recognizing that for my team, organization, family or business to go beyond where they presently are requires my personal growth is at times intensely challenging. You must examine the leadership culture in you. That which you possess will largely sculpt the culture in which you're a part. An example is if you are typically late or procrastinate, the culture that you are creating is a culture that will disrespect the time of others, as well as your own. Developing the Leadership Culture in you requires discipline and is necessary in many areas, but three are essential: Time Management, Structure and Resources.

1) Time Management
Self-leading in the area of time is fundamental to successful leadership and creating a leadership culture. Effective leaders efficiently use their time and are self-aware of their effectiveness. A mentor challenged me on the effective use of my time. He introduced me to the concept of "time blocks." The idea is to set the most important aspects of what you do in the most effective time slots in your life. For instance, if you are highly energetic and sharp in the early mornings, then your high pay-off activities need to be engaged during those hours. If you are sluggish in the afternoons, then that is when you schedule activities that require less of your emotional and mental sharpness.

What are your most effective times of day?

What are your high pay-off activities?

What adjustments do you need to make to prioritize those activities with your most effective times?

*Be the change you want
to see in the world.*

(Gandhi)

2) *Structure*

Self-leadership in the area of structure is crucial to the development of a healthy culture. In order to create a leadership culture the leaders must live a lifestyle that fosters leadership. Leadership cultures attract leaders; bureaucracies drive leaders away. A leader must bring on those he can entrust to be subject experts and give them the freedom to function. Telling someone what to do is different than telling them how to do it. The leader should set the vision and allow others to help the organization by using their gifts, creativity and energy. A leader who manages will create bureaucracy which will disperse leaders.

As a leader, if you can't resist telling competent people exactly what to do then you must self-lead toward change. If you are telling them exactly what to do because they don't possess the leadership to execute, then you must replace the individual or manage them. If you choose to manage them, then you are creating a culture of bureaucracy.

A non-leader requires management because he is a reactive employee, reacting to leadership. A leader requires empowerment because he is a proactive employee, a part of leadership.

A bureaucracy's purpose is to compensate for incompetence. In order to create an effective leadership culture, one must self-lead and self-evaluate what type of culture they are creating through their own actions and dispositions. The goal is to create a structure that you manage while not managing the people. Help everyone to understand the purpose, values, and structure and what their role is in accomplishing the whole and then let them go with great goals.

What kind of a culture do you demand? Do you create?

Does your culture require a lot of rules, guidelines and procedures in order to produce work from those in leadership? What does this mean?

Will your environment attract leaders in the future? Why or why not?

What is your course of action?

3) *Resources*

Self-leadership and resources are intertwined. In order to create a leadership culture one must first self-lead with regard to resources. Self-leadership must set the standard to "fund the vision." Put your money where your heart is. The key to effective resource spending is understanding your DNA.

Jim Collins, in his book *Good to Great*, describes what he calls a "hedgehog" concept. That is "what you can be best at" in conjunction with what drives you economically as well as what are you passionate about. He describes successful organizations as having discovered one thing that they can be best at and focusing on that particular area with passion. I call this DNA.

The DNA of an organization is a combination of Purpose, Pay-Off and Passion.

First, identify your Purpose as an organization or ministry. Why does it exist? What is it designed to be? What is it at the core? **Describe.**

Second, identify your organization or ministry's Pay-Off activity. What product or service could you absolutely not survive without? What's your economic engine? **Describe.**

Third, identify your Passion. For some this might be success, excellence, service or money. **Describe.**

These three make up your DNA. You should resource toward your DNA.

> *If your resource strategy is incongruent with your declared vision, then you are delusional.*

At Grace Point Church, the church I serve, we have identified our Purpose as "leading common people into uncommon life in Jesus." Identifying our Pay Off activity is simply an "exchanged life" or "grace lifestyle" which are people who recognize and live out their identity in Christ. The characteristics that are displayed in a Christ-follower are the 5 Gs: grace, growth, gifts, give and go. Our Passion is Jesus, his church and telling others about Him.

In our context we recognize that we must staff toward the vision which requires great leadership. We resource to leadership. We also resource toward the strategy areas that lead to mission measures being embodied in our congregation.

Resources are scarce and must be prioritized around what is most crucial to the company or community's DNA.

The self-leadership lesson is that you must lead by example. It requires you lead change in your own life and thinking in order for the organization to experience health.

What do you feel is the leadership culture of your present organization in the area of time?

In the area of structure?

In the area of resource?

What must you personally grow in order for your organization to grow?

Decision Making

Decision making is a barrage of impulses, frameworks and contexts. The cultural message is that truth is relative and therefore make decisions based on how you feel. The problem is that if we have led for any amount of time at all, we know that this is hazardous. There are times when we've made good decisions and others when we have made bad decisions. But what is the right approach?

We as human beings are made up of physical, emotional/mental and spiritual properties. In decision making it is essential to understand how these three aspects of who we are interplay and the flow by which we make good decisions.

At the core of our being, we are spiritual. We have a design that causes us to relate to God or to long to relate to Him. Next, we have a mind, will and emotions through which we process information for us to act upon. Finally, we have our physical body, by which we act through speech, hand gestures, walking, etc.

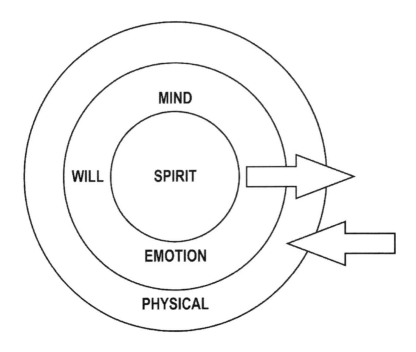

There are two ways to make decisions: outside in or inside out.

Outside In: When we make decisions from the outside in, we allow external circumstances or events to overwhelm us, and then we have feelings about those circumstances from which we drive thoughts. These thoughts then are developed from logical frameworks, previous programming or personal philosophy. If we are spiritually alive, our spiritual point of reference will then in turn react to the entire process, a filter which may or may not catch the decision already produced. If we are not spiritually alive, then we are incapable of making decisions from this vantage point.

Outside In decision making works like this:

- "What I heard her say sounded harsh." (physical, sensory response)

- "That makes me feel angry. I don't deserve that tone or attitude." (emotional and mental response)

- "Lord, give me the grace to respond in an appropriate way." (spiritual if alive and sharp)

Inside Out: Making decisions from the inside out assumes and requires spiritual consciousness. This is to be spiritually alive and consciously living from a dependence upon God's Spirit within you. From here, you adjust your mind, will and emotions. Then you physically respond based on the internal flow of the spirit which has provided the framework from which to think and feel.

Inside out decision making works like this:

- "Lord, I am yours. May your Spirit guide and direct my mind, will and emotions, as well as the work of my hands." (spiritual consciousness is primed before encountering external stimuli)

- "Lord, I will filter my life through your Word." (mind, will and emotions subject to an objective standard—love is a choice, not an emotion)

- "Lord, I will speak and do that which is consistent with your will and your Word." (ordering your physical actions in light of your spiritual direction)

From here, when you encounter the harsh words the initial stimuli is internal, not external. You are prepared and working from your spiritual center. All great decisions are made from here.

Do I typically make decisions Outside In or Inside Out? Describe.

What does it require of you to make decisions starting with your spiritual center, from a submitted and surrendered state?

Do you filter decisions through the framework of scripture? Describe.

Developing a Decision Matrix

1) *Submission to the Holy Spirit*
Beginning with the Holy Spirit, it is important to be certain that all decisions are made from a submitted state. Business decisions that are quick and capricious even though they are intuitively and instinctively right can be tragic when the Spirit of God is divorced from the equation. Personal decisions almost always are doomed when disconnected from the Spirit's voice. The Holy Spirit is the first and most effective filter in all decision making.

2) *Dependence on God's Word*
Most of the ethical principles in business and otherwise can be traced back to Judeo-Christian culture. God's Word is effective whether you're a believer or not. If you are a believer, then this is a certain cross check for what you believe the Spirit is telling you. The Spirit will not tell you to do something that Scripture says not to do.

3) *Seeking Wise Counsel*
Who are your mentors, wise counsel, board of advisors in decision making? When making a decision, especially a major one, it is important to use your mentors as a sounding board. Mentors are like physicians. You will have some who are general physicians, but others who are specialists. Bill Hybels, in his book *Courageous Leadership*, breaks his mentors down into Risk Assessment Mentors, Performance Mentors (those who guide and influence how you handle the performance of others), Excellence Mentors (those who   influence your standard and where it should be placed), and Morale Mentors (those who influence how you encourage, motivate and inspire). These "specialists" influence your decisions just by the

thought of "I wonder what ___ would do."

4) *Experience*

Experiences, good and bad, shape our decision making, but shouldn't shape it in total isolation. That is why these other filters must be consulted first. Experience, when used in conjunction with the rest of your matrix, will be a powerful decision making tool and likely the most concrete. Hybels call this his "pain-file." Experiences both good and bad provide a powerful context from which to lead. When our experiences are filtered properly through our decision matrix, we have a great opportunity to decide well and as a result lead well. We should always remember and yet not be enslaved by the past.

Who are your mentors?

Who is your General Practitioner?

Who is your Risk Assessor?

Who is your Excellence Mentor?

Who is you Performance Mentor?

Who is your Morale Mentor?

Revisit Purpose Statement

You have completed both the *Foundational Leadership* and *Self Leadership* sections. Take the opportunity to go back and refine your purpose statement and resolutions.

Notes:

TEAM **LEADERSHIP**

LESSON SIX: Team Purpose and Values

Team

As we move from "foundational and self-leadership" issue, which define our purpose, values, resolutions and goals, we have the framework from which to apply leadership in other areas of our lives. The concentric framework of leadership will now move from the individual outward to family, corporation, regional and even national influence.

Review

- My Personal Purpose Statement:
My destination. "I exist to…"

- My Values:
The way or character with which I will pursue my destination.

- My Resolutions:
  The obvious clear strategic values and priorities that are related to my purpose/destination. "Therefore, I must…"

- My Goals:
  Dynamic measurable goals in order to pursue my resolution and ultimately my purpose (destination). "Therefore, I will…"

The personal process is the foundation framework from which to lead others. You cannot take someone somewhere you have never been yourself. Once the personal process has been laid you can now lay the foundational framework for the team you lead.

First, process these questions:

Who am I leading?

What team am I responsible for?

What organization or group am I a part of that needs a leader

> *A team cannot share values until the values are shared by the team.*
> (John Maxwell)

Team's Purpose Statement
We exist to...

Team's Resolutions
Therefore, we must...

Team's Goals
Therefore, we will...

Team Values

Team Values are the character with which a team is going to pursue the Purpose established. Team Values must reflect the values of the leadership. While these values may be somewhat different from the personal values you have previously developed, they will most often be complimentary if not synonymous.

What are the essential values for your team?

How are they different from your personal values?

How are they complimentary or synonymous?

Recognizing Team Values are values that are held by the leadership, it is important for the leader to develop these values. A leader, however, must also recognize that there are values held by those who work alongside the leader that must be heard and embraced. These two truths are not exclusive to one another and must be delicately worked through.

Establishing Team Values
In order to establish team values, first, list all the values you believe your team should possess. Then ask your team to do the same. Take all of the lists and cross reference them with your list and see if other values can fit within the values list you have created. Then take the values that did not fit into those on your list and evaluate whether or not they are crucial to successfully arriving at the purpose.

Make a master list showing where you have incorporated other values into those stated on your list plus the others stated (these are the values that don't fit into yours but that you recognize may be essential).

Realizing that there are a limited number of values that you can successfully live out, ask your team to prioritize a top ten list. Now they have evaluated the list and prioritized, you have evaluated their suggested values that may differ from yours and at this point it is possible to come up with values that your team can embrace and embody.

Which values made the list that weren't on your original list?

Are you pleased or perplexed by these emerging values?
(It is important to identify how these affect you since it is crucial for you to embody each value.)

Incorporating Team Values
In order to incorporate team values these values must first have a strict definition. You must define whatever term you use. The next key to incorporating values is that they must be memorable. Sometimes developing a "tag line" encompasses the definition. There are different ways to develop corporate language but the key is that it becomes part of the fabric of the team.

An example of one of our values as a church is "Relationship." The definition is "ruthlessly pursuing authentic interaction, selflessly putting others first and passionately loving from a point of grace." The tag line is "Mind the Gap!"

Develop a short, strict definition for each of your team values.

What will make each value memorable?

Things that make values memorable include: tag lines, contextualizing them, transferability, ability to napkin test them, visibility in environment, celebrated when embodied, disciplined when violated and consistently incorporated into all evaluations.

Maintaining Team Values
In order to maintain these values, they must be celebrated through both recognition and reward. These are powerful ways to reinforce the values that your team possesses. Never underestimate the power of a public "atta boy." As we begin to reward what we value, we reinforce the values that will carry us toward our purpose.

The reward system must not be tied to that which we do not want perpetuated. For example, you have a team member who adds to your bottom line, but doesn't do it with integrity or the right attitude, etc. If your rewards system is tied to the bottom line, then you are reinforcing that team member's behavior for your team.

Describe your rewards/recognition system and how it supports your values.

Enforcing Team Values

Values enforcement is crucial to the good of the team. If values aren't enforced, they cease to be held. If values are capriciously enforced for some, but not for others, they will cease to be held.

Our Relationship value's tag line "Mind the Gap" means if there is a gap in relationship between me and someone else, I am responsible to bridge that gap. Team members will come to me upset with another team member and my advice to them is "mind the gap." This is not something generally people want to do, but when gaps are minded issues get resolved.

Enforcing the values make the values come alive. The other side is true as well. Team members have been asked to no longer be on the team because of a refusal to embrace and embody the values. While this is difficult, it enforces the values.

Are your values clear?

Are your values held?

Are your values enforced?

Embodying Team Values

Initially we mentioned how crucial it is that the values that the team possesses originate with the values of the leader. While they may not be the same as the leader's stated personal values, they would be consistent with or synonymous to those values. The reason this is so crucial is that team values must be embodied by the leader.

What values do you possess that, if you were honest, do not possess you?

Who has the right within your team to enforce a value in your life?

Embrace vs. Embodiment
Embrace is holding to a set of beliefs as true, embodiment is living out those set beliefs to the point of being associated with them. The question is, does your team associate you with the held values? In my experience, one of our team values is Encouragement, defined as "joyfully and enthusiastically encouraging others in their pursuit of God." I embraced this value as essential and even wrote the definition and presented the value. The problem was while I encourage from time to time, my team did not associate encouragement with me. This continues to be the value that I work most diligently to embody.

The bottom line is if the leader doesn't, the team won't (whether the team is home, business or church).

Identify which value is your greatest challenge.

How will you begin to embody that value?

On-Boarding Team Values

On-boarding means that every new team member must be methodically taken through a process that helps them to embrace, hold and embody the values the team possesses. "Sink or swim" mentality is detrimental to the team and the individual. There must be a process to ingesting the values. Many leaders focus on events to communicate values to team members. For example, a wedding is an event, but it does not make a good marriage. A good marriage requires the right information before the wedding, the right mindset during the wedding and the right tools implemented after the wedding.

When is the best time to on-board a new team member?

What is the best process? What does it look like? What do you need to adjust to what you are currently doing?

How will you maintain the energy behind the values with your current and ongoing team members?

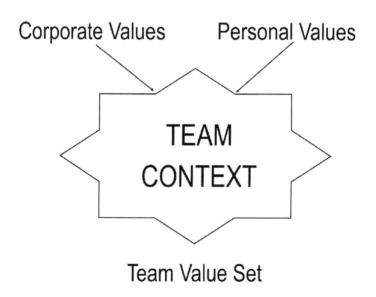

Corporate Values   Personal Values

TEAM
CONTEXT

Team Value Set

Notes:

LESSON SEVEN: Teachable Point of View

Teachable Point of View (TPOV)

Whether you know it or not, you possess a Teachable Point of View, in fact you likely operate and possess many. This is an idea or outlook that characterizes the way you approach life, work, or relationships. The object is to develop your Teachable Point of View so that it benefits your team and becomes an overriding philosophy, concept or value. A potent form of communication efficiency, the art of refining TPOVs empowers a leader to influence and rally teams to a way of operating with remarkable clarity.

Noel Tichy explains Teachable Point of View in his book *Leadership Engine*. "Having a teachable point of view is both a sign that a person has clear ideas and values and a tool that enables him or her to communicate those ideas and values to others. It is not enough to have experience; leaders must draw appropriate lessons from their experience, and then take their tacit knowledge and make it explicit to others. This requires not only that they have a point of view in their own minds, but that they can explain or teach it to others." The goal is to make a TPOV your own so that you are able to package it, put a handle on it and teach it.

Developing a Teachable Point of View

What idea or dream evokes passion in you? What makes it teachable?

What would people most likely want to learn from you? What is the danger of not passing that knowledge on?

How does this idea relate to your purpose (destination)?

Why is this idea important? How does this idea honor God?

Write down one to three of your Teachable Points of View.

How do you make them portable? Do they have tag lines?

Share your TPOVs and record reflections/responses from others.

TPOV Examples:

Don't Play Chess
Speak honestly, get to the real issue now. Don't try to manipulate and

shroud your agenda. Put things in the open. Now. (General)

No Drama in Trauma
In crisis situations, all personal drama and snares need to be put away for a calm focus on the patient and present crisis. The operating room is too critical of a time to have surrounding drama distracting the team. (Hospital)

Process is Slave to Purpose
Never marry the way something is done beyond the why it is done. Processes are great, but they are disposable in light of the driving goal of purpose. (General)

Bill Hybels' book *Axiom* is a series of organized TPOVs.

Quantum and Incremental Ideas

Noel Tichy also defines Quantum and Incremental Ideas. Quantum Ideas set a direction for everyone. They are big, overriding principles that set direction and are essential to keeping everyone working toward a common goal. Incremental Ideas are about strategy, structure and implementation. They are dynamic, specific actions that are taken to reach the Quantum Idea. You need both. Quantum ideas provide the framework on which incremental ideas hang, and incremental ideas shape the actions that get the quantum ideas implemented.

An Example:
A manager of an electric company has a teachable point of view of going directly to employees of all levels for ideas. This manager had the quantum idea that the electric company could be more cost-efficient by increasing the utilization of his assets—the service trucks. He asked the service truck drivers

for incremental ideas on how to get this done. As a result, the electric company changed the way they dispatched trucks. The incremental idea of service truck drivers driving the trucks home at night eliminated unnecessary trips to the garage, adding almost two hours of productive workday.

Quantum Ideas are also connected to your purpose (destination). It is a vehicle or tool by which to communicate and fulfill your purpose.

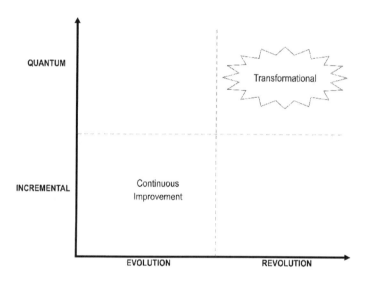

Developing Quantum and Incremental Ideas

A Quantum Idea of mine is the concept of "Dynamic Ecclesiology." In keeping with my purpose to lead the Church, it is the idea that in order for the Church to function biblically, it must be free to dynamically change its form so long as the biblical functions are being fulfilled.

The specific Incremental Idea within this Quantum Idea is title changes. At our church, we do not call servant leaders deacons, we call them Point Persons. We found that the term "deacon" lent itself to the concept of authority or ruling and in order to return the role to a more biblical function, we changed the term and fulfilled the role.

Having the freedom to change the form but fulfill the function is the Quantum Idea, and the change of the specific role and terminology is the Incremental Idea. Take an idea and tweak it!

These are some brand statements that underscore a Quantum Idea. Can you guess what the Quantum Idea might be?

"Have it your way."

"Wheels Up!"

"The customer is always right."

"People, People, People."

What are one to three of your Quantum Ideas?

What is required to see these ideas fulfilled?

What are the implications of not developing these ideas?

When you compare or bench mark with others (families, corporation, etc.), what distinguishes your method, philosophy or process?

Notes:

LESSON EIGHT: Infusion

Infusion

The team dynamic requires a leader to display personal focus on the purpose, the quantum idea, as well as the values and goals. Infusion is the energy and determination of the leader that is poured into the team members. This energy is required to fuel the team dynamic.

If a leader is sporadic with his attention toward the purpose, values, goals and quantum, then he becomes the chief source of distraction from those essential elements. If a leader lacks the determination to fight through difficult circumstances or lacks the courage to make difficult but necessary decisions, then his team will stagnate.

Infusion plays itself out in personal focused determination, enthusiasm, inspiration, personal sacrifice, and seizing teachable moments during change.

Read Mark 14:32-41. Jesus is about to be arrested and ultimately crucified. Just prior we find this scene with him praying to God the Father in a garden. What was Jesus trying to infuse into his disciples?

Read Matthew 10:5-42. Jesus had only been with his disciples for a few months, perhaps a year and is sending them out on short-term missions. As you read the instructions of Jesus, what was Jesus trying to infuse into his disciples?

Personal Focus

Personal focus is a leader's ability to remain constant and pursue what matters most. There are several questions you must answer with regards to your own personal focus:

Are you a sprinter or a marathon runner?

Do you lose interest once you've started or established momentum? Where do you lack consistency?

What mechanism do you have in place that is required for your ongoing focus? What triggers do you need to put in place?

Does your team expect your consistent focus or do they wait for you to lose passion?

The answer to these questions may help you in discerning where you can work on your personal focus. If you are sprinter, then you need mechanisms in place that ensure your ongoing focus. Failure to recognize and compensate for such tendencies as a leader will incline your team to simply wait for you to lose interest.

Determination

While personal focus speaks to consistency, determination speaks to the will. Determination is the leader's ability to push through difficulty and adversity while focusing on the purpose, values, quantum idea and goals.

Does your team see you as determined?

How do you handle defeat or setbacks?

Do circumstances affect your enthusiasm? What steals your passion?

Do you avoid tough choices?

The answer to these questions will help you to grow in the area of infusion because your determination directly affects the will of your team. If there is 'quit' in you, there will be 'quit' in them.

Read Luke 9:51. As you read the context of this passage you'll note that Jesus is facing considerable opposition. How does Jesus' determination have implications on you as a leader?

Enthusiasm

Another aspect of infusion is enthusiasm. As a team leader it is important that you provide the emotional energy as well as the vigilant character your team requires. Your enthusiasm directly affects your team. If you are excited about a direction, product or event, they will be excited as well. If you lack enthusiasm for something that is necessary, or that you as a team have decided to do, then your team will lack enthusiasm. You will deflate any enthusiasm that might have existed if you yourself aren't enthusiastic.

Once I assigned my staff a book I had not yet read. We had a reading schedule and I pitched the book as something that we needed and could benefit from. About two weeks into the book I had totally lost enthusiasm. It wasn't that the material in the book was bad. We did need the information, but the way the book was written left me listless. My team soon was having a hard time with the book also. My enthusiasm, or lack thereof, crushed any momentum we may have initially had.

What is the difference between being excited and being enthusiastic?

Are you an enthusiastic leader? Explain.

Are you behind what you are leading? Do you believe in it?

How have you noticed your lack of enthusiasm affecting others?

How can you keep yourself enthusiastic?

Don't buy shoes from a
barefoot salesman.

Inspiration

Inspiration is crucial to effective team leading because it motivates your team toward something larger than themselves. A vision and purpose that is larger than us is inspiring. Inspiration has the power to breathe life into an idea or direction, it fans the flame of hope and passion. It says, "What we are doing counts!"

Do you call people to something larger than themselves? "What would it look like for..." or "What would it mean if you..."

Do you believe their lives are more significant now that they are a part of this team?

Sacrifice

Sacrifice is a team leader's obligation and privilege. Sacrifice is the intrinsic character of a leader. It states that "I am willing to pay the cost because I believe in our purpose and values." It means that you will not ask your team to pay a price that you are not willing to pay. Leadership through sacrifice knows no entitlement, and models the commitment necessary to succeed.

What are you sacrificing for the good of your team? Does your team view it that way?

What equals sacrifice to your team? What does it look like to them?

Read Matthew 4:18-22. What does Jesus call these men to that would make them leave everything?

Teachable Moments

Another aspect of infusion has to do with seizing the teachable moments. As a parent, I recognize how important it is not to let time pass between a behavior event (good or bad) without explaining to my kids the significance of that behavior. Teams need real time feedback. When someone hits a home run, they need to review what they did right. When someone wrecks what do they need to do to reflect on what they didn't do right. As a team leader, we must seize these moments and teach. We cannot simply applaud or reprove—we must seize moments in order to improve!

Where have you witnessed real time feedback done successfully? How about unsuccessfully? What were the results of both?

How effective are you at real time feedback?

Are you too far removed from the people that need your wisdom most?

Do you find yourself rewarding and disciplining or teaching? Explain.

You set culture interaction
by interaction

Success is often a self-correcting
condition... We too often mistake
the edge of our rut for the horizon...
Even a successful rut becomes
hazardous to leadership edge and
purpose over time. (Gary Hamel)

Change

The final aspect of infusion is change or tension. John Maxwell says, "if you need no change, you need no leader." When your team is at the height of success the tendency is not to change a thing, but the truth is—change is crucial.

People may feel unchallenged, they become difficult to motivate and your own leadership is at risk. Infusing strategic change or tension at the right time causes the team to respond and continue to strive and move forward toward the purpose. Change and tension move us toward the purpose, not away.

Are you in a rut of any kind? Family, business or church? Describe.

What change could you make that would stimulate that area?

In what area do you not have problems?

What change could you make that would stimulate that area?

Who is your most dependable, steady team member? How can you challenge him or her?

Notes:

MULTIPLYING **LEADERSHIP**

LESSON NINE: Identifying, Investing In & Entrusting

→ → → → → → → → → → → → → →

Great leaders multiply. Leadership is often said to be determined by "is anyone following?" And while this is an important assessment feature, it can be equally said that leadership can be determined by multiplication. To turn and see someone following is addition; to develop those followers to develop followers themselves is multiplication.

Are you presently *adding* or *multiplying* leaders?

If you are only adding, why?

As we look at multiplication, there are certain critical features that are required and the first of these is learning to *identify* emerging leaders.

Identifying Emerging Leaders

In identifying emerging leaders, selection and response is a simple yet profound truth.

Read Mark 1:14-20. What was Jesus' appeal? Was he recruiting to a job/task or to a mission?

Was Jesus' appeal an addition or multiplication appeal?

Leadership development
never happens accidentally.
(Bill Hybels)

1) *Response*
Response is crucial to developing multiplying leaders. Often we have hired or recruited individuals that we thought were going to be the greatest asset to our team. Soon we are discouraged and disappointed. We have all experienced the nightmare of

bringing on the wrong person. Jesus invited the rich young ruler to follow him as well, but the person with seemingly the most potential was unwilling to do the first most critical step and that is to respond. Jesus modeled the resolve of a mission-oriented leader to not short-circuit the response of potential team members despite general qualifications.

Who in your organization is responsive?

Who, despite their potential, is unresponsive?

What gauges of response do you use?

2) *The 4 C's*

The second key aspect of identifying emerging leaders is selection. Selection is crucial to the success of our teams. In hiring we should follow the 4 C's: character, competency, chemistry and calling.

Why would each "C" be important?

Character:

Competency:

Chemistry:

Calling:

In identifying leaders, we must develop a characteristic list. It is important for you to think critically about what is crucial to great leadership. Develop a top 5 leadership characteristic list. I will share with you the one our team developed.

- Character: *Displays integrity and ethos.* (Psalm 78:72)

- Positive Desire: *Has a positive attitude and passion.* (Psalm 119:139)

- Teachable: *Is a life-learner and is coachable.* (Proverbs 1:8)

- Influence: *Has magnetism as witnessed by having followers.* (Matthew 4:19-20)

- Discipline: *Displays consistency and possesses essential daily practices.* (Luke 9:23)

Work on your own list. Some of the characteristics listed may be on your list, but you might define it somewhat differently. The key is that you and your leadership team reach consensus on what it means to be an effective leader in your context. This will help you in identifying those that you want to pour your life into. If you assess that an individual does not possess some of these traits, then you must evaluate whether or not you should be investing in them for the purpose of leadership.

List Your Top 5 Leadership Characteristics:

3) *Emerging Leader List*

The next critical step is to develop an emerging leader list. Take your key leaders that you already have in place and based on the leadership characteristic list, identify individuals in the organization who have leadership potential. Be careful!

Who is displaying potential?

Who has the raw goods, but needs refining?

Who has been sidelined and why?

Lists of emerging leaders must not be static, as people are not stationary in their development. How do you refresh your list and awareness of diamonds in the rough?

Some people should not be a leader, and part of effective leadership is discerning such to protect the team and mission.

Who presently is in a leadership role in your organization who doesn't possess the essential characteristics?

What is your plan of action? (Necessary change is a leader's obligation.)

Investing in Future Leaders

We know that great leaders multiply. Multiplication however doesn't just happen. Having identified an emerging leader list as well as developing the characteristics of a leader, you are now prepared to invest. Investing in emerging leaders is central to leadership development. No successful movement or organization can sustain its vision apart from consistent, intentional investment in future leaders.

Read Luke 22:7-15. Jesus is just 48 hours away from ending his earthly ministry. There is much yet to be done, so many things He could be doing with this last window of time. What strikes you about Jesus' choice and instruction here?

Investing is crucial to the advancement of your team, but most leaders spend more time with non-leaders than working with potential leaders. Leaders are often doing well and so we spend our time on those who need the most instruction or crisis management. Investing is a paradigm and behavior shift. We must spend 80% on the top 20%! Once we identify the top 20% of our leadership base, we should now invest 80% of our time, energy and resources.

Identify your top 20%.

Read Matthew 14:13-21. This is a famous story, but note closely...How many did *Jesus* feed?

How many did Jesus invest in for future leadership?

How much time do you spend developing leaders? (in hours/week)

How much time do you spend with non-leaders trouble shooting, instructing or crisis managing? (in hours/week)

.

List all the reasons that 80% on the top 20% is not possible for you.

List the cost of not investing 80% on the top 20%.

List the consequences of not developing leadership.

Principles of Investing

1) *Expectations*

We must first answer the question "What's required?" for those we will lead. We need to let them know what our expectations are going to be for them. We need to clearly line out our expectations so that there isn't doubt or interpretation. The next thing we must do is to tell them "What's reachable." This is to vision cast them for the future potential that you see in them. You must let them know what it means to be a leader, but also what you believe is going to be accomplished through their leadership. You must tell them what you see in them.

Read Matthew 19:21-30.

What does Jesus tell them is required in verse 21?

What does Jesus tell them is reachable in verses 28-30?

Complete this statement for your leaders: "I see in you..."

2) *Opportunity*

The next principle of investing is opportunity. We must point out the opportunities and raise them to a level to seize the opportunities in front of them. Investing is moving your people from one opportunity to the next. Providing and enlightening opportunities along the way.

In Mark 6:7-13, how does Jesus provide opportunity for his future leaders?

In order to set your team up for success, you must point out the opportunities around them. Never underestimate the importance of an early win!

What opportunity were you given that changed your life? Who gave you that opportunity?

How are you different today because of that opportunity you were given?

3) *Feedback*

The third principle in investing is feedback. We must regularly dialogue with our leaders on how they are doing, what they can do better and how they can grow.

The feedback cycle is as follows:
- Approach regularly
- Dialogue
- Inquire
- Evaluate
- Teach
- Equip
- Hold accountable

Read Luke 10:17-24. The disciples have just returned from their short term trial mission trips. Did Jesus follow the feedback cycle? How?

Do you have a process to give your leaders feedback? Where do you need to start? What practical steps are you going to take?

4) *Coach*

The fourth principle of investing is coaching. Coaching is simply positively guiding them as needed. Along the way, as a leader emerges, you will spend less time in the feedback loop, but you will always provide encouragement along the way. Your goal should be to develop your leaders to the point that they are self-leading, but from time to time approach you for individual coaching.

We have been looking at the leadership process of Jesus in our own understanding of investing.

What is the coaching equivalent from the Biblical perspective?

How do you receive ongoing coaching from Christ? Did Christ see ongoing coaching as important?

Who is providing ongoing coaching for your team?

Who is providing ongoing coaching for you?

Read John 14:25-27. What are the implications for you as a leader?

5) *Recognize*

Recognition is crucial in investing because it understands that each person must be validated equal to or greater than their contribution. Recognition is the investment of encouragement. We all need validation and encouragement. In leading others, it is imperative to acknowledge their contribution and at times go beyond recognizing their contribution. Setting your team up for success and recognizing that success is a leader's greatest investment.

Read Matthew 26:6-13. Who is Jesus recognizing?

In what degree—equal to or greater than her contribution— did Jesus recognize the woman? Why do you think he went to such lengths?

How are you recognizing your leaders?

Do you struggle with encouraging them by recognizing them beyond their contribution? Why?

How can you develop this as a part of your regular leadership investment in others?

Entrusting Leadership to Others

Multiplying leadership requires us to entrust leadership to others. Entrusting is a key issue in all effective leadership. As we look at entrusting we must also recognize entrusting is NOT abdication of responsibility or even mere delegation of responsibility. Entrusting is passing the torch. When we entrust we have passed through identifying and investing and now we are prepared to turn over leadership.

Read John 21:15-20.

Jesus' final days were spent preparing His disciples to receive the mantle of leadership. As we look at this level of entrusting, we will see certain paradigmatic precursors that prepare leaders to be entrusted.

Precursor to Entrusting

1) *Give and get commitment*

Entrusting is about empowering others to lead themselves. This is a sacred trust that must be respected. This requires the present leader to give and get commitment from the leader who is emerging. The give aspect is to tell the emerging leader what he or she can expect from you. The get aspect is to receive from the emerging leader an agreed upon commitment of what can be expected of him or her.

In the Jesus/disciples relationship:
- Come follow me / fishers of men
- Leave homes and families / 12 thrones of Israel
- Holy Spirit comes upon you / you will be my witnesses

When we give and get commitment, we establish the ground of our relationship. In biblical terms, this is a covenant. "Believe in Me and you will be saved." In leadership terms, this is a relational contract. Without a give and get commitment there will be frustrations due to unspecified and unmet expectations.
- "Serve in this manner and you will become a partner."
- "Exhibit these skills and you will have your own franchise."
- "Grow in this manner and you will teach your own class."

Do you have a clear give and get commitment with those you are developing for leadership?

2) *Vision and career path*

The next entrust precursor is to lay out the vision and career path so that the emerging leader can see the major peaks on the landscape. This should be out of their comfort zone, but not out of their gift zone.

Read Matthew 16:17-19. What is Jesus' vision statement for those that follow Him, confessing He is the Christ?

Does this sound like delegation or entrusting?

3) *Growth Goals*

In conjunction with their career path, emerging leaders should be given growth goals that identify strengths, abilities and attitudes. These are areas that they need to grow towards. In the area of strengths one needs to pursue a career path that is in keeping with these strengths. If you have an emerging leader who is not gifted or strong in a certain area, it is possible for him/her to succeed as a leader, but it may not be in this particular area.

George Barna's research indicates that while pastors are in leadership positions, 8 out of 10 don't possess leadership gifts and skills. I remember in my preaching class in seminary when our professor stopped a fellow student in the middle of his third sermon and said, "You don't have to do this to yourself, there are plenty of ministry opportunities that don't involve preaching sermons in a public setting." I remember the look and tears of relief as this future leader realized he didn't have to conform to some generic mold.

Attitude is crucial. In order to entrust we must discern and dissect right and wrong attitudes. A growth goal with a right attitude is easy, we simply affirm and challenge the emerging leaders to develop and spread this attitude. When the attitude is in need of adjustment the growth goal is to grow towards change and usually this involves a paradigm shift.

Read Matthew 18:1-6. What attitude adjustment was Jesus instructing his leadership team on in this passage?

The attitude was wrong, so the paradigm was changed. We cannot make the light bulb come on with attitude goals, we can only make sure the bulb is new and the plug is connected.

The Cost of Not Entrusting

I have been a part of two church plants. Both required lots of money and time as well as the entrusting of key relationship to unproven leaders. I can tell you I spent many hours in frustration and in anguish simply because the precursor steps were not clear. The consequences were painful and costly. My own fear of entrusting is that it will cost a relationship or will cause the standard of excellence to be lowered. I believe the consequences are that people won't come to Christ because of our ineffectiveness. My personal response was to do it myself. My realization is that I will never reach as many alone as I can reach through identifying, investing, and entrusting other leaders.

Entrusting

Identify when and where. When the emerging leader is ready, the opportunity must be identified and the leader deployed. Timing is critical. To send them too early will be painful and to send them too late is equally painful. At this point, they are as prepared as they are going to be and it is in everyone's best interest for them to fly.

Expect multiplication. Each leader that you entrust should be commissioned to multiplication. The investment is now to be reciprocated in the ongoing development of others. The ongoing coaching relationship should focus on multiplication in the deployed emerging leader.

Here's the disturbing reality: you are here because someone chose to invest in you with an intent of multiplying leadership. You likely got to where you are today because of many others who had the same mindset. If you do not translate these principles into how you lead, if you do not entrust, then the buck will stop with you. Does your purpose demand more than a one hit wonder? Our mission certainly does!

Notes:

Closing Thoughts

Reflect

What are your biggest take-aways, the biggest impacts this experience has had on you?

What have you done with this material so far? What have you already begun to do differently?

What will you do or implement later? If you were contacted a year later, what will you have implemented?

Thank You

Leadership is not about position, title or function-it is about influence. In your setting, are you influencing it out of the reality of your purpose and make-up or are you the victim of it? Do you impact your surroundings or are you shaped by them? That's the core essence of leadership that precedes the higher tactics of formal leadership. Lead where you are.

Thank you for investing in your own leadership quotient by being part of the Leadership Forum experience. You were identified on purpose, you participated in a purposeful process and my prayer is that you will go forth leading and growing with a purpose in all areas of your life.

Appendix

LESSON ONE: Why Do I Exist?

1. There is a Chinese church planting strategy based around teaching simple truths and not advancing beyond any lesson until application has been embodied. What was found was that by the time just a few lessons were completed the participants were ready to begin planting their own churches. It was a testament to the fact we tend to consume way more information than we discipline ourselves to apply/employ. What would happen if as a leader you actually implemented the wealth of principles and knowledge you already have? That's why the Leadership Forum experience is a process of application.

2. The Bible says followers of Jesus are called to be "salt" and "light" in the world. Neither are passive or neutral elements.

3. http://www.fastcompany.com/magazine/140/do-something-wordplay.html

LESSON TWO: The Importance of Values

1. For examples of applying this same exercise to your home life in particular, request a copy of *Family on a Mission* from Grace Point Church.

LESSON THREE: Goal Setting

1. Remember that resolutions are timeless, but goals are incremental ways of advancing or achieving them.

2. Goals are not predictions they are targets.

3. A helpful presentation on categorical goals and their inter-dependencies can be found at http://www.slideshare.net/emailgoldie/goal-setting-using-zig-ziglars-life-wheel

LESSON FOUR: The Leadership Compass

1. Self-leadership is very similar to discipleship, in that you cannot minister out of an empty cup nor can you lead others in a pursuit you are not engaged in.

2. Bill Hybel's book, *Too Busy NOT to Pray!* Is a good resource

3. When evaluating "The Call" it is valuable to consider the distinction between a corporate and individual calling. Also a general call versus a special revelation call. For example, whether or not a father feels called to a job he has a general call to provide for his family.

4. In the exploration of gifts, resources such as Strength Finder 2.0, Leading From Your Strengths and the SHAPE test are excellent diagnostics.

LESSON FIVE: Leadership Culture and Decision Making

1. Having a clear picture of the core elements of your organization are is critical to identifying where resources and investment should be channeled. At Grace Point, we utilize a concept called the Vision Frame (consult *Church Unique* by Will Mancini) that captures the essence of our mission, strategy, measures and values. From clarity of what our vision frame is we are then empowered to say "no" to the myriad of nice things that come along that are not truly to mission.

2. *A Game Plan for Life* by John Wooden is a good resource on the concepts of mentorship

LESSON SIX: Team Purpose and Values

1. *Values Driven Leadership* by Aubrey Malphurs, *Get Everyone in Your Boat Rowing in the Same Direction* by Bob Boylan are great resources on creating and instilling team values

2. USAA, Valero and Rackspace are dogged about threading every communication, review and announcement through the lens of values

3. Some excellent presentations on application of team values can be viewed at:

http://www.slideshare.net/reed2001/culture-1798664

http://www.leadership-and-motivation-training.com/developing-team-values.html

http://dhavalpanchal.gettingagile.com/2008/07/15/sharing-values-a-team-building-exercise/

LESSON SEVEN: Teachable Points of View/Quantum Ideas

1. Coach Bill Walsh was famous for his TPOV of "West Coast Offense," which is derived from the Quantum Idea of a running/passing game mix and the Incremental Concept of strong receivers (big/fast).

2. Other examples of TPOVs include: Obedience Precedes Change, Go to Grow, PUSH (Persistently Urge Staff Higher), Tertium Quid (no false dichotomies), and Know and Be Known.

Consult *The Leadership Engine* by Noel Tichy for a full exploration of these concepts.

LESSON NINE: Identifying and Investing in Leadership

1. Ask your facilitator for a copy of the Grace Point "Character to Lead" assessment as a sample instrument for assessing leader candidates.

Bibliography

Axiom, by Bill Hybels

On Becoming a Leader, by Warren Bennis

Gung Ho, by Ken Blanchard

Fish, by Ken Blanchard

Good to Great, by Jim Collins

Principle-Centered Leadership, by Stephen Covey

Leadership is an Art, by Max Dupree

Servant Leadership, by Robert Greenleaf

Primal Leadership, by Daniel Goleman

Courageous Leadership, by Bill Hybels

The Leadership Challenge, by Kouzes and Posner

The 21 Irrefutable Laws of Leadership, by John Maxwell

The 17 Irrefutable Laws of Teamwork, by John Maxwell

The Performance Factor, by Pat MacMillan

Ordering your Private World, by Gordon McDonald

The Ascent of a Leader, by Thrall, McNicol and McElrath

The Leadership Engine, by Noel Tichy

Spiritual Leadership, by J.O. Sanders

StrengthsFinder 2.0, by Tom Rath

Becoming a Person of Influence, by Maxwell and Dornan

The Tipping Point, by Malcolm Gladwell

The Top Ten Mistakes Leaders Make, by Hans Finzel

Who Moved My Cheese, by Spencer Johnson

Jeff Harris has served as the Senior Pastor of Grace Point Church since 1994. Under his leadership, Grace Point has transitioned from a traditional church plant into a growing, dynamic community of believers that is transforming the surrounding community and world. He is a graduate of Baylor University and Dallas Seminary, and has four children with his wife Jody.

.

Made in the USA
Lexington, KY
16 March 2017